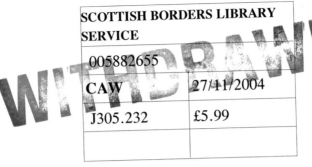

First published in Great Britain in 2004 by
Cherrytree Books, part of the Evans Publishing Group,
2A Portman Mansions
Chiltern Street
London W1U 6NR

Copyright © this edition Evans Brothers Limited 2004

Originally published under the title
'Mes Petites Encyclopédies Larousse Le Bébé'
Copyright © Larousse/VUEF 2003

Text by Agnès Vandewiele

ISBN 1 84234 262 2

A CIP catalogue record for this book is available from the British Library

Printed in France

ALL YOU NEED TO KNOW ABOUT...

Babies

Illustrated by **Anne Wilsdorf**

CHERRYTREE BOOKS

Important news!

Mummy and daddy
are happy.
Mummy is pregnant,
she is expecting a baby.

6

Will it be
a girl or a boy?
Will it have
straight fair hair or
dark curly hair?
Will its eyes be
blue, brown
or green?

You can't choose,
it will be a surprise!

7

Where do babies come from?

First of all, there is a mummy and a daddy who love each other very much. They want to have a baby.

When a sperm from the daddy joins up with an egg in the mummy it makes an embryo, which will grow into a baby in the mummy's womb.

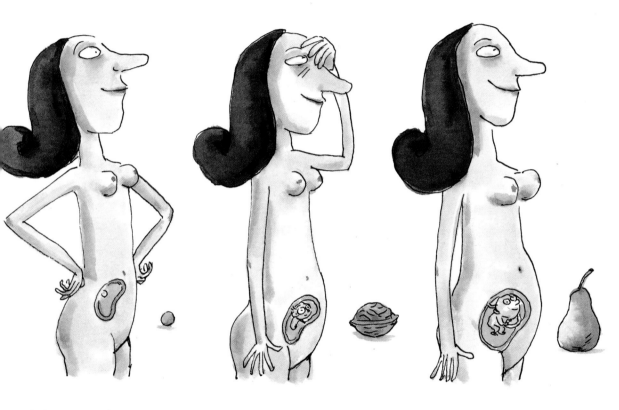

The womb stretches as the baby grows. At first the baby is the size of a pea.

Then the baby grows to the size of a walnut.

After three months the baby is as big as a pear.

The wait

Sometimes mummy is tired
and needs to rest.

There is a lot to get ready
for the new baby.

When will the baby be born?
In nine months – what a long time to wait!

As the baby grows, mummy's tummy gets bigger. She needs some new clothes.

Watching baby grow

The doctor has a machine that can show pictures of the baby in the mummy's womb. He can check that the baby is growing properly. He can also see if it is a boy or a girl.

Sometimes there are two babies – twins.

At four months, mummy can feel the baby move inside her.

At five months, the baby's hair and nails grow. You can feel him kicking.

At six months, the baby sucks his thumb. Sometimes he has hiccups. He grows even more!

Mummy and daddy think of names for the baby.

Like a fish in **water**

The mummy's womb is a bit like a big bubble filled with a liquid, called amniotic fluid. The baby floats in the fluid, which protects him from bumps and germs. The fluid is renewed all the time.

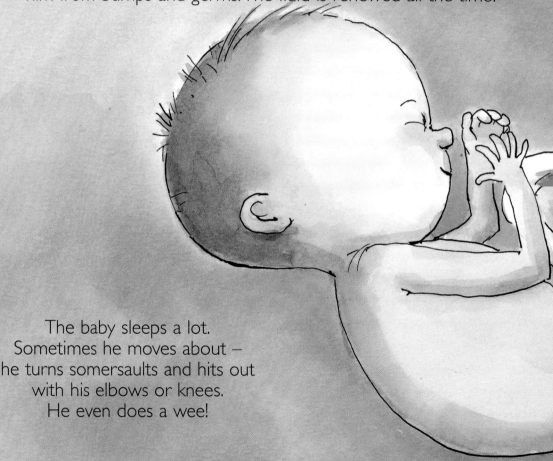

The baby sleeps a lot.
Sometimes he moves about –
he turns somersaults and hits out
with his elbows or knees.
He even does a wee!

A long tube, called an umbilical cord, joins the baby to his mummy. Everything the baby needs to help him develop goes along the tube.

Sometimes the baby grabs hold of the cord. He might stroke it, or pull it, or suck it — it's his first toy.

Mummy eats all kinds of things so the baby can grow strong.

Three months to go!

At seven months, the baby recognises voices. He can open his eyes. If his mummy gets close to a bright light, the baby sees it and jumps!

At eight months, the baby turns upside down. He is getting ready to be born. Mummy gets ready too: she goes to special classes to help her prepare.

At nine months, the baby has grown so much that there is hardly room for him to move. Mummy's tummy is also very big.

Everyone in the family gets ready for the baby.

They buy a baby basket,

baby clothes,

nappies and a changing table.

Grandma knits little outfits.

The nursery is ready.

And so is the family!

17

The birth

Night or day,
the baby decides
when the time
has come.

Mummy can feel
in her tummy that
the baby is ready
to be born.

Off we go
to the hospital!

At the hospital, the midwife or the doctor
is there to help with the birth.
This can last for several hours.

Look, the baby has arrived! He makes his first cry.
He breathes for the first time. His skin is a bit wrinkly.

The first moments

The newborn baby rests on his
mummy's tummy for a few minutes.
It's his first cuddle!

The doctor cuts the cord because the baby doesn't need it any more. All that's left is a little mark, called the navel.

The doctor tests the baby's reflexes.

A nurse weighs and measures the baby.

If the baby is born too early, or if he is very small, he is kept in an incubator while he grows a bit more.

Daddy learns how to wash the baby…

and how to dress him.

A beautiful baby!

Mummy stays in the hospital for a few days with the baby.
The baby gets to know the rest of the family.

Everyone wants to see the new baby, and brings little presents.
But who does the baby look like?

Daddy tells their friends the good news.

He takes lots of photos for the album.

The baby's birth is registered. His date of birth, and first name and surname are written in a book.

Life as a **baby**

A new baby sleeps a lot and is often hungry.
At first, he wakes up every three hours, even at night,
to suck milk from his mummy's breast or drink from a bottle.
When he's finished he has to give a little burp.

The baby has a
bath every day.

His nappies need to be changed
several times a day.

A baby likes to hear people talking
to him, and recognises the voices of
his mummy and others in the family.

Careful! A baby is fragile.
You need to hold his head
when you pick him up.

Mealtimes for baby

A new baby doesn't have any teeth. He only drinks milk.

He has to get used to new tastes. Sometimes he pulls a face and turns away.

At about six months, the baby starts to eat mashed vegetables and stewed fruit.

He drinks water and fruit juices.

At about eight months, he starts to eat a little meat mixed in with the vegetables.

But he can't hold a spoon yet!

27

At the **doctor's**

During the first few months, mummy and the new baby have to visit the doctor several times.

The doctor weighs and measures the baby to check that he is growing bigger and stronger.

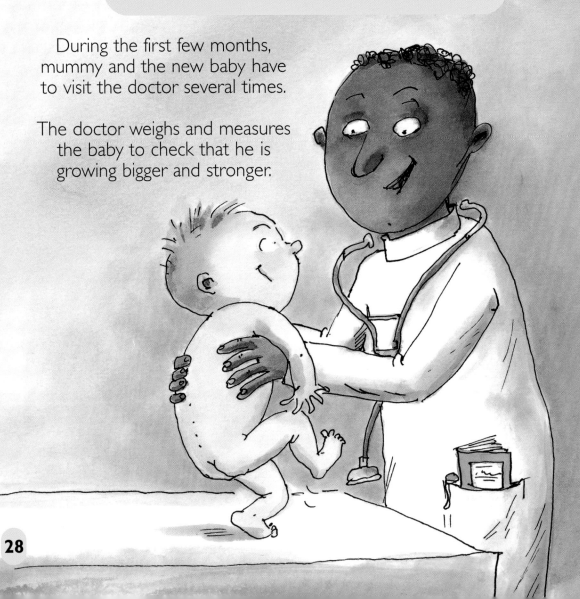

28

The doctor listens to the baby's
heart and breathing.

He vaccinates the baby to
protect him against some illnesses.

The baby cries when he is
hungry and when he is tired.
Sometimes he cries a lot…

Perhaps he has earache,
or a cough, or spots.
That means he is ill and
has to go to the doctor's.

The first year

A baby changes every day.
Little by little he learns how to do new things.

At one month, he smiles when he sees your face. He holds your finger very tightly.

At about four months, he holds his head up and makes gurgling noises.

At six months, he can just about sit up. He grabs hold of everything he can reach!

At about eight months, he can sit up well all by himself.

He starts to crawl and explore the house.

At about one year, he starts to pull himself up onto his feet. He says his first words.

Baby likes to be **busy**

If mummy and daddy work, a baby might go to a crèche or a nursery.

Or he might be looked after by a nanny during the day.

At the swimming pool, the baby likes floating in the water.

He can go everywhere with daddy in his baby carrier.

In the car, he has his own special baby seat.

In the pram or pushchair, the baby can watch the world around him. There's always plenty to see in the park.

Baby likes...

to be held…

to be cuddled…

playing in the bath…

playing peek-a-boo
with his brothers
and sisters…

and throwing his
toys down for
someone else to
pick up!

When he's happy he
smiles and gurgles.

Baby doesn't like...

loud noises…

sudden movements…

dirty nappies…

or being left alone
somewhere new!

If he's not happy, he cries.
But it's not always easy to
know why a baby cries.

It's true!

Very **tiny**

At two months, the embryo in the mummy's womb weighs only a few grams.

When the baby is born, he weighs more than 3 kg, that's 1000 times more!

Very **heavy**

During her pregnancy, a mummy puts on 10 to 12 kg, the same as the weight of a two-year-old!

A beautiful **baby**

A newborn baby weighs just over 3 kg and measures 50 cm.

A big **head**

A baby has a very big head –
about one-third of the size of his body.

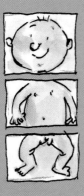

A big **family**

Very rarely, a mummy has several
babies at once. They are born
one after the other.

A big **appetite**

A newborn baby needs to be fed
five to eight times a day.

A big **sleeper**

A newborn baby sleeps for
sixteen hours a day.
He wakes up to eat.